Hello and welcome to the start of your Fire Up! Journey.

I am so thrilled you are here!

We are going to share a magnificent adventure of self-discovery, personal development, and business building.

It is no accident you chose this book... you are ready.

xxoo,

SHOUT OUT AND PRAISE

Debra Trappen and
Fire Up! Taking Your Life and Business to 11

"Debra is 100% authentic - she lives and breathes her personal brand and her story. She isn't a speaker or writer who talks about one thing and does another. She truly walks the walk. She is also one of the kindest people I know but is also completely straight-forward and will tell you like it is - to bring out your personal best!"

- Katie Lance
Founder * katielance.com

"Debra is one of the few people I can go to when I am in a funk or need advice and immediately feel like I can accomplish anything. There are so many influencers that are not positive or humble and that is what Debra personifies. I am blessed to call her a friend and a mentor. She is a "what you see is what you get" gal and that is so needed in today's business world."

- Lisa Archer
CEO, Trainer, and REALTOR® * livelovehomes.com

"Hands down the best advice for living your authentic self & expressing it in your own way. Learn how to engage on social media platforms & taking those relationships to the next level, offline. Debra infuses you with endless inspiration, this book is just the beginning of an opportunity to brand your business in creative ways that you've been missing. It's simple, sassy & straight to the point branding advice for any busy professional. "

-Carol Farrar
CEO/Broker Owner * 1850Realty.com

"Debra's real life passion and authenticity shine bright on every page! I felt the author was sincerely engaging and guiding the reader to help them discover their "Why".

Debra has a fun, feisty, effective way of getting you to look inside at your core values, passions, branding, defining your ideal client, social media strategies and much more... all so that you can better serve your customers/clients but staying true to yourself all along the way!

If you are looking to be INSPIRED and "Fire Up" your business, I highly recommend you read this book."

- Lori VanDinther
REALTOR®/Team Leader * loriv.com

"This book is a GIFT to me at this point in my life (as I am completing my doctorate) and I recommend it to everyone and anyone who desires to be EVERYTHING to EVERYONE! We are expected to LOVE all people, but it is not expected that we pursue THEIR paths as if they were our own! So grateful for this book, its wisdom and Debra's enthusiastic writing and inspiration throughout! I am ready to change my world!"

- Paige Evans, Educator

"I love the very clear tips and tricks. It is very clear on what I need to do to take action on and what I need to implement now. I literally read this book on the plane (there and back). It was easy to digest and challenging all at the same time. I put the book down at one point and sent a note to my team on something to execute on Monday morning. That is a good read. I have known Debra for over a decade and her message is consistent and what she preaches in this book she lives!"

-Shandel Slaten Sutherland, Coach-Author-Entrepreneur

Fire Up!

Taking Your Life and Business to 11

By Debra Trappen

Foreword by Rebekah Radice

Published by e5 publishing
Copyright © 2015 by Debra Trappen
Second Edition Published 2017

ISBN 978-0-9961194-2-9

FIRE UP CONTENTS

FOREWORD

PEEK BEHIND THE SCENES

INTRODUCTION

WRAPPING IT UP

FIRE UP YOUR MOXIE

RESOURCES

This book is dedicated to my faith-filled, bold, supportive, and loving husband, Andrew.

Along the way, his servant heart, patience, and genuine, deep love have lifted me up, inspired me, and grounded me.

Special thanks to my Pops and Queen Mum... Being raised in a God-centered home by an engineer with a passion for sci-fi and a power women entrepreneur with grace and passion for others has shaped me into the woman I am today.

I am forever grateful for the love and support that surrounds me

FOREWORD

When Debra Trappen asked me to write the foreword to her book, "Fired Up! Taking Your Life and Business to 11...," I was thrilled. Having known Debra both offline and online for several years, I know what a remarkable woman she is.

Our first introduction was through social media. It wasn't until some time after that when we finally met face to face. I remember it as if it were yesterday. I walked into an opening night cocktail party at the Inman Connect Real Estate Conference in San Francisco. There, in the middle of the room, surrounded by at least a dozen women was Debra.

I quickly crossed the room and snuck in a hello, not wanting to interrupt the hubbub that her presence had inspired. After our initial greeting, which more than likely included a hug and many squeals of delight, I listened in as Debra mesmerized her crowd of adoring fans. Now when I say mesmerize, certainly it could be over her beauty. Whether you know Debra online or off, you can't help but notice her stunning good looks. Who could miss that fiery red hair? Her hair seemingly puts the spark in her spunky and always memorable banter.

Debra is so much more than that. She captivates the crowd because of her ability to speak to the very core of what makes us all tick. So while she's beautiful, she's also brilliant, charming, charismatic and extremely knowledgeable when it comes to fusing passion with human communication.

Debra has an innate capacity to take any situation and turn it into a moment. And making the most of each and every moment is the very essence of Debra's life mission.

Her teaching is practical and actionable, giving you the tools you need to not just live life, but also give flight to a life you have only seen in your dreams.

This book contains everything you need to stop dreaming and start doing, to stop surviving and start thriving. Every section of this book contains proven steps and strategies that Debra has used to help others get from where they are, to where they want to be. Her book is a testament to her years of work identifying what holds us back in life and how to shed those limiting beliefs and step into a positive, productive and profitable mindset.

Now, let me warn you. If you're looking for coddling, handholding or someone to tell you that staying in your comfort zone is ok, you have come to the wrong place. You're also not going to find any fluffy anecdotes or convoluted theories. Debra's a straightforward, tell it like it is, no-nonsense gal. Her approach is a breath of fresh air and one that has resonated deeply with me since the day I met her.

My hope is that you'll gain as much from this book as I have. That you'll walk away inspired and empowered to make the necessary changes within your own life and business. I know that through Debra's skilled instruction, you will be able to push through the tough stuff, the not so fun stuff, but the stuff we all have to work through to truly know success, no matter what that looks like to you.

I know that if you commit to following the book through, from beginning to end, you will come out on the other side having uncovered a whole new you!

Rebekah Radice
Award Winning Marketer
Author, Social Media Mastery:
A Comprehensive Guide to Social Media Growth
rebekahradice.com

PEEK BEHIND THE SCENES

It was truly my heart's desire to write a valuable, entertaining, and practical life guide to help you clarify and amplify the elements of who you are... what I call your Core Four! Through the years, I have mentored hundreds of people with this technique to help them define and design the best version of themselves. When you start with YOU first, it brings clarity to every decision ahead – whether it is about family, your career, starting a business, saying YES to the best events and no to the ones that don't serve your purpose or align with your values – and so much more.

You will find ooooooodles of exercises, moxie-filled tips and truths, and Fire Up! case studies and stories shared inside this easy read.

For the reader "on-the-go": You can easily read this on a flight between Los Angeles and New York City and it is light enough to pack along in your handbag or carry-on to revisit and review the process along the way! To get the MOST out of the book, on round one, do the exercises as you go.

You will also find signature, sassy labels and concepts inside this book. Here are the highlights and their "definitions":

- o What is up with the number 11?
- o What does "Take It To 11" mean?
- o What is a #MoxieMemo?
- o What is a Fire Up Story?

What is up with the number 11?

People often ask me these questions and I love it. The number 11 is part of my story and sharing "why" always ignites me. So, here it goes:

My love of 11 went to an 11 when I met my amazing husband. I was living in apartment #1111 – he was living in #11. We were engaged on 11/11, married on an 11th and celebrate every 11th - every month. When we see 11:11 it reminds us to slow down and connect to one another, and count our blessings.

Friends and family – both online and off – associate the number 11 with me. Friends from all around the world send screenshots of their phone at 11:11, when they are sitting at table 11, when they are at exit 11 - you get the idea. It has become my "Social Object", that "thing" outside of a logo, name, or photo that reminds people of me.

(Hmmmm... do you have a social object?)

What does "Take It To 11" mean?

In my life and business, the number 11 is a reminder to stop, think about what is happening in that moment, and challenge myself to take the EXPERIENCE to the next level. Add a little extra "something" to make what I'm preparing, creating, or engaging in even more remarkable, memorable, and even truly unforgettable.

This book is all about guiding you through the process to taking your brand, business, and LIFE to an 11, too!

My mission is to inspire you to ask yourself:
- What can I do today to "Take It To 11"?
- Who can I call, write, or visit and take their day to an 11?

When you find those opportunities – snap a photo and tag it #FireMeUp11 to inspire others on the journey!

What is a #MoxieMemo?

You will also notice me sharing something called a #MoxieMemo. These are short, succinct quotes or truths to FIRE YOU UP, get you out of your own way so you start living your best life, and embracing your greatest potential! If you are inspired to share one please include the hashtag so I can see it and engage with you!

What is a Fire Up Story?

Throughout the book you will be reading stories from clients, colleagues, and friends sharing their Fire Up! journey experiences. We all love to read and share our stories. The stories of struggles and successes INSPIRE us to push farther and dig deeper, so these amazing people stepped up to do that for you!

If you want to reach out to anyone mentioned, please feel free to tweet me @debra11 with the #FireMeUp11 hashtag and I will get you connected!

I look forward to engaging with you at one of my workshops, at a conference, retreat or event, or in the social media streams!

How will you wrangle all of your information along the way?

You can use a journal, notepad, or app on your device to collect the info.

I also put together a digital workbook you may download here, as you wish:
http://debratrappen.com/fireupworkbook

INTRODUCTION

"Shine your fiery light. Share your REAL journey.
When you are courageous, you create a spark that ignites
and inspires others to be brave!"
~Debra Trappen

Hello, and welcome to the start of your Fire Up! Journey!

I am so thrilled you are here and that we are going to share this magnificent adventure of self-discovery, personal development and business building - TOGETHER!

You are amongst your tribe here.

- You wake up and **KNOW** there is more.
- You **BELIEVE** you are worth investing in.
- You **SEEK** to be surrounded by **CHAMPIONS** and are always nurturing those relationships.
- You **EMBRACE** a "Why Not Me?" attitude.
- You **EMPOWER** others with "Why Not You?" encouragement!

You are in the right place at the right time!

Now, I want to be very clear - **you are about to get REAL with yourself.** When you stop and think about it - nearly all of our research, development, and learning is about what is around us. What is outside of us; what we can SEE, TOUCH, or FEEL.

The Fire Up process is all about self-discovery and introspection. Defining what is UNSEEN and profoundly important to uncover.

Your Fire Up journey is all about discovering and clarifying what is INSIDE YOU and then leveraging it to help you build a life and business that is beyond your wildest imagination!

When I sat down to write this book, and the subsequent workshop and eCourse, my heart's desire was to create a guide to help you start and maintain your personal Fire Up journey.

This book is where
personal development meets business.

While the Core Four elements and exercises you will go through are universal, the second half of the book is truly written for **independent sales professional and solopreneurs** – those whose personal brand is a KEY element in their company's brand and growth.

For example, if you sell real estate, mortgages, or financial services; are a consultant, coach, trainer, author or speaker; or are part of a multi-level marketing/network marketing company this book is written for YOU.

If personally or professionally standing OUT in a "sea of same" in digital, networking, and lifestyle marketing is something you struggle with or are ready to take to the next level – you have chosen this book... **wisely**.

My vision behind the chapter order and design was for you to read through the book – cover to cover. It is a perfect 3-hour flight read since usually takes people about that long to consume the entire book. Now, if you are a speed-reader or have multiple distractions like technology or toddlers nearby, this estimate may be way off. (wink) Regardless, once you have read through the book – THEN go back and revisit (or do) the Core Four exercises.

You will hear me refer to "personal brand" throughout this book. For most people, some of the biggest challenges with personal brand are: simply understanding what it is, why they need it, and how they build one.

Let's start by tackling three questions.

1: What Is Personal Brand?

Personal brand is a specific image or impression in the mind of others about YOU.

It is the words people use to describe you, online and offline; the things that remind them of you and the way you make them feel. It may include words, topics, attitude, colors, numbers, clothing, etc. that trigger YOU in their mind - these are elements of your "personal brand".

The elements of YOU!

2: Why Do You Need It?

First of all, let's be clear - you already have a personal brand. It is less about **why** you need it and more about embracing your ability and responsibility to define and nurture it. You knowing YOU is important, wouldn't you agree?

A strong personal brand can be the difference between mediocre success and extraordinary success - both in life and business. As an independent sales professional or small business owner marketing your professional services and products, building your industry influence, growing your sphere and email list, or improving and nurturing your credibility online - you are marketing yourself so those people you want to connect with can FIND YOU.

Do you know the answers to these questions?

- What am I doing to inspire others to read and listen to my messages or use my products and services?

- How do I convince them I am right for a project?

- How am I the best resource for them - what is my relevant, valuable offering?

Personal brand is being authentically and freely YOU.

This is your opportunity to share your vision of who you are, what you love, and what you uniquely have to offer the world. If you don't define and share your personal brand and story, you are allowing others to determine what you are all about, what you do, why you do it, and ultimately share their version of you.

3: How do you design a personal brand?

Designing a strong personal brand starts with focusing in on your "Core Four" Foundation:

1. Defining Your Personal Core Values
2. Filling Your Soultank
3. Uncovering Your Life's Purpose
4. Creating Your Niche Statement

You are defining and stating who you are, who your ideal clients and connections are, and how you are the solution to their problems.

Once you clarify, and consistently share your Core Four, you start to build influence and a connection with those people you are equipped to and desire to serve.

#MoxieMemo: *A solid, fired up personal brand will attract the ideal people, opportunities, and success to you - like a magnet.*

SUCCESS (and we will define what that means to you in a future chapter) is sitting on the other side of your comfort zone.

Are you ready to move towards success and start your personal brand journey?

Are you ready to get uncomfortable to become unstoppable?

The next several chapters include a deep dive into each of the Core Four Elements to get you on the path to a clear, concise personal and brand foundation that you are confident about – from the inside out!

I believe you are ready...
and I dare you to believe it too!

Chapter 1
Define Your Core Values

"The thing I love most about core values is their ability to ground you. You never have to wonder if a decision is the right one or if that client is well aligned to your business. Your core values are your guiding light."
~Rebekah Radice

The first element in your Core Four is your list of core values! It's time to put your 5-point harness on and get this journey started by defining your core values - also known as your personal principles!

Stating your core values
is like embracing a SUPER POWER.

When you value something, people recognize it. People see and believe it. Passion and enthusiasm may open the door, however a clear vision and defined values will fascinate your audience and inspire them to build a relationship and partnership with you. Solid values attract clients who share the same mindset as you do... and are essential to your personal brand.

Values are your compass. They point to the things you deeply believe are important in the way you live and work.

They ultimately assist in determining your priorities and are how you measure if your life is turning out the way you want it to... or has gone off course.

When your actions align with your values, life is usually smoother and your drive comes from abundance, not fear or scarcity. However, when your actions don't match up, decisions and things feel "off". This can be a real source of depression, dissatisfaction, and general uneasiness.

If you don't know what's important to you, you waste precious, limited time wandering and wondering what you could, would or should be doing.

Core Values help you determine how and with whom you spend your time.

Are you living your values or are your choices forcing you to live out of alignment?

Do you find yourself making statements that SCREAM you are living outside your values?

Statements like:

"I haven't had time to meet up with and connect with loved ones in weeks." *(Values Out of Alignment (VOA): Relationships)*

"Workout or sit down to eat? When? I rarely have time for that!" *(VOA: Healthy Living, Fitness)*

"I can't remember the last time I had a quiet moment to myself." *(VOA: Alone Time, Introspection, Peace)*

"My schedule is so crazy. I haven't seen my children or tucked them in for days!" *(VOA: Family)*

"My house is in chaos - the dishes and laundry are piling up as I speak!" *(VOA: Aesthetics, Excellence)*

"I know I need to, however I haven't been on a vacation in a very long time." *(VOA: Adventure, Fun)*

If you are nodding your head thinking – YES, I have said some of those things (or a lot of them) you are NOT alone.

Shame. OFF. You.

Shake it off. NOW is the time to stop, reevaluate, prioritize, and finally GET REAL with your fab self!

The truth is "Defining Your Values 101" is not part of the general curriculum in school. For many, no one spells it out or helps you outline what you really want when you grow up. We graduate, jump into a career, marriage, family and then, one day, wake up feeling off – way off.

Ooooooodles of people talk about "values". They remind you to live by them and run your homes or businesses by them, but don't share the magic pill that grants instant clarity.

This is such an exciting time for you! Why, you ask?

I believe when you fully understand and
operate from your values...
MAGIC HAPPENS.

Your values come alive in ways you would never have imagined. **Clarity around your values guides you to:**

- Make decisions more confidently
- Choose connections more intentionally
- Live your life out loud more often

How can you be sure that your actions are aligned with your truest self? *You define and live by them, so let's get started!*

Fire Up Step 1: Define Your Values

Look over this list and choose your top 11 words.

- ❑ Abundance
- ❑ Accountability
- ❑ Achievement
- ❑ Adaptability
- ❑ Adventure
- ❑ Aesthetics
- ❑ Ambition
- ❑ Authenticity
- ❑ Awareness
- ❑ Balance
  (home and work)
- ❑ Being liked
- ❑ Being the best
- ❑ Caring
- ❑ Caution
- ❑ Clarity
- ❑ Coaching and mentoring
- ❑ Commitment
- ❑ Community involvement
- ❑ Compassion
- ❑ Conflict resolution
- ❑ Continuous learning
- ❑ Contribution
- ❑ Control
- ❑ Cooperation
- ❑ Courage
- ❑ Creativity
- ❑ Dave or city
- ❑ Dialogue

- ❑ Ease w/ uncertainty
- ❑ Efficiency
- ❑ Enthusiasm
- ❑ Entrepreneurial
- ❑ Environmental
- ❑ Ethics
- ❑ Excellence
- ❑ Fairness
- ❑ Faith
- ❑ Family
- ❑ Financial stability
- ❑ Forgiveness
- ❑ Friendship
- ❑ Future generations
- ❑ Generosity
- ❑ Global awareness
- ❑ Health
- ❑ Honesty
- ❑ Humility
- ❑ Humor and fun
- ❑ Inclusiveness
- ❑ Independence
- ❑ Initiative
- ❑ Innovation
- ❑ Integrity
- ❑ Interdependence
- ❑ Job security
- ❑ Listening
- ❑ Logic
- ❑ Making a difference
- ❑ Mission focused

- ❑ Open communication
- ❑ Openness
- ❑ Patients
- ❑ Performance
- ❑ Perseverance
- ❑ Personal fulfillment
- ❑ Personal growth
- ❑ Personal image
- ❑ Positive attitude
- ❑ Power
- ❑ Pride
- ❑ Professional growth
- ❑ Quality
- ❑ Recognition
- ❑ Respect
- ❑ Responsibility
- ❑ Risk taking
- ❑ Risk-averse
- ❑ Safety
- ❑ Self discipline
- ❑ Simplicity
- ❑ Success
- ❑ Trust
- ❑ Uniqueness
- ❑ Vision
- ❑ We Ward
- ❑ Wealth
- ❑ Well being
  (physical/emotional/ mental/spiritual)
- ❑ Wisdom

18

Now, enjoy the process of choosing YOUR words!
Remember, if you prefer, you can access the exercises
in a workbook: debratrappen.com/fireupworkbook

**Once you have your 11 values chosen and prioritized,
add them here:**

1.

2.

3.

4.

5.

6.

7.

8.

9.

10.

11.

To start getting them intentionally woven into your
days, weeks and months – print out your list and post
it somewhere you will see it every single day. *The
bathroom mirror, inside your closet door, taped to your
nightstand – wherever works best for you.*

For the next few weeks, take a look at your list every night before you go to bed. Review it. Revel in the values you lived aligned with and note where you were not in alignment.

This simple sheet will help you keep track, as you wish.

Week 1 * Values Check In

		S	M	T	W	T	F	S
1	_____	☐	☐	☐	☐	☐	☐	☐
2	_____	☐	☐	☐	☐	☐	☐	☐
3	_____	☐	☐	☐	☐	☐	☐	☐
4	_____	☐	☐	☐	☐	☐	☐	☐
5	_____	☐	☐	☐	☐	☐	☐	☐
6	_____	☐	☐	☐	☐	☐	☐	☐
7	_____	☐	☐	☐	☐	☐	☐	☐
8	_____	☐	☐	☐	☐	☐	☐	☐
9	_____	☐	☐	☐	☐	☐	☐	☐
10	_____	☐	☐	☐	☐	☐	☐	☐
11	_____	☐	☐	☐	☐	☐	☐	☐

1. Why are some of my words being honored and represented while others are not?

2. What will I do differently next week?

3. What 3 values do I want to focus on next week?

4. What activities will help me achieve this goal?

Fire Up Step 2: Create short, fire up statements

In my Fire Up! talks, courses and workshops, we go through a process of creating "Fire Up Statements" for each one of your values.

Craig Groeschel calls these "Life-Giving Statements" in one of his leadership podcast. He shares, "If you can't tweet your values, they are too long. If your values don't move you emotionally, they are too dry. If your values don't move you to action, get some new values."

The goal is for our personal, core values to be memorable, portable, evoke emotion, and inspire action in US.

Fun formula to follow:
CHOOSE Your Value Word + **DEFINE** An Action You Can Take + **DECLARE** What You Will Experience

Here is an example:
I honor my value and practice of well being (my value)
+
by daily infusing plenty of water, walks, prayer-filled meditation and sleep (my actions)
+
so I am able to grow old and thrive with my beloveds! (my WHY)

Ready? Time to write one of your own!

Fire Up Step 3: Practice P.E.A.C.E.

Now, it is time to put them into practice. Before you say YES to an invitation to have coffee, become a volunteer, partner on a new project, or attend an event, etc. review these steps:

1. **Pause:** Take a moment to answer any request.

2. **Examine:** Ask yourself: "Does this opportunity align with my values?"

3. **Assess:** Review your goals…. Which one does this get you closer to achieving?

4. **Choose:** You now have the option to choose wisely. Not every single decision you make will fit perfectly into your value structure, but when you use this process you are consciously aware - from the start.

5. **Execute:** Now you can confidently and intentionally, integrate the activity, nurture the relationship, etc. knowing it will add value to your life – in alignment with your core principles.

Doesn't that sound marvelous?

Now, let's look at a couple of practical examples.

Example 1: You Value Positivity

A friend or colleague invites you out for coffee. Before you reply to an invitation to meet, ask yourself:

1. Does this person consistently bring positive energy to the conversation, talk about how she is overcoming/embracing a business challenge and thrive on sharing her connections to build strong businesses - together? OR...

2. Are you coming home from your coffee connect with a sour attitude because "Mr. Toxic" just spent an hour complaining about his life, marriage, job, clients, etc.?

Do you see how clearly this should be a NO reply?

Example 2: You Value Healthy Living

You want to eat better, cleaner, and local. Before you go shopping, ask yourself:

1. Do the stores you shop in align with your values, either by philosophy, ingredients, sourcing locations, or experience standards?
2. Are the items in your basket going to get you closer to your health goals or the meal plans you have designed for my family?

You want to infuse healthier options into your schedule and create an evening routine. Before you commit to events, ask yourself:

1. Do the time and activities of your commitments match your values? For instance, if you want to add in meditation, yoga, exercise, writing, reading, or even more sleep – look closely at your commitments.

2. Do they align and support your goals? Can you move a couple dinner meetings to breakfast, lunch or an afternoon coffee chat so your evenings are freed up for more personal development time or sleep?

3. Can you switch food centric or happy hour meetings to "walking meetings"?

   BONUS: These walks will also help with a "financial freedom" value, too, since you aren't spending money on expensive food and drinks.

An additional, FANTASTIC benefit to getting clear about your values is you will get more confident and comfortable saying NO!

NO.

This word is actually a complete sentence. Go ahead - say it out loud.

NO.

Doesn't that feel amazing? Many of the most successful people on the planet say NO way more often than they say YES. It's time to embrace their mindset. **If it doesn't align, it's a NO!**

Fire Up Step 4: Review And Refine

As you get into the groove of infusing your values, put them to the test.

Be sure to pay attention to when, where, how, and with whom you are living in alignment with these words.

Make sure those words you chose are the RIGHT ONES, too. There is no rule stating your values won't change along the way. I have seen values shift with major life events. For instance, healthy living or well being usually shows up - or rises in priority - on your values list when a health crisis hits. Go ahead and shift them around and replace words, as you wish.

These are YOUR VALUES.

Core Values will also show themselves differently throughout the years...

Adventure may be ranked in your top 2 in your 20's and may involve weekly camping and hiking trips; in your 30's it may be building forts with the kiddos in the living room - on the weekend; and in your 50's it may be traveling Europe or taking a month long river cruise.

Can you see how this is showing up in your life?
As you learn more about yourself, you will start to see how you are living your values more and more every day. You will be inspired to weave then into every decision you make and every project you take.

Fire Up Story:

The first story I want to share with you is from Tina Mitchell. Tina and I met when I was speaking at a Women's Council of REALTORS® meeting in the Seattle area. She was the sponsor of the meeting, so after connecting there – we decided to meet for coffee. Tina was immediately intrigued by the Core Four process and jumped in the process with all her heart and soul.   il took time to really think about what was important to me and what I credit my success to. For me it was to dream, be alert and learn to fail. I also wrote quotes on each of my core values that I could read everything so to really embrace them.

Dream, Inspire, Appreciate, Compassion, Strength and Integrity

Next step was the realization that is not just ok but a must for my business to share my core values in my business. This was difficult for me at first as I felt my core values were for me and me only. I didn't think it was appropriate to bring them into my business. Was I ever wrong about that?

Once I committed to be the person I was in private and share that person in public did the real magic begin. I noticed that my clients and business partners had the same core values and interest that I did. It opened up an entire new business for me.

Live your dream now, inspire others, appreciate the small things, show compassion, have strength to pull through it and live with integrity.

It is YOUR TIME to define your values, infuse them into your decisions, and embrace your super powers.

Stating
your *values*
is like embracing a
superpower!

Chapter 2
Fill Your Soultank

"Passion is energy. Feel the power that comes from focusing on what excites you." – *Oprah*

The second element in your Core Four is to get in touch with what you are truly passionate about – right now.

First, let me explain what I mean by your "soultank"?
I imagine we each have this sweet space inside us that fills up when we are doing things we love. It is a source of energy, patience, and joy.

Each of us experience **"soul moments"** in our lives that **FIRE US UP and fill our soultanks!**

Those moments include activities we love, charities we are passionate about, people we adore being with, things we love to surround ourselves with – and we want to experience these moments *as often as possible*!

The challenge is we get rolling with work and the responsibilities of life and forget to stop and fill our own tank.

When your soultank is empty, you are not living up to your true potential or tapping into a divine happiness that belongs to you – not to mention you are not serving others at your highest level.

When I start talking about this, most people can't even remember the last time they thought about how full their soultank was. Working to take the time to recognize and feel where you are right now is such a fantastic exercise.

Knowing what ignites a spark inside you or elevates your mood "sounds" simple. However, many people, especially servant-hearted professionals like you, do not slow down long enough to think about these things – let alone define or infuse them.

If you don't define what you have genuine passion for in your life, you will never fully convince or inspire people to partner with you, work with you, or join your movement.

Start by simply asking yourself:

- Am I content and joyful, right now? or...
- Am I an exhausted cranky-pants even I would avoid?

(The latter is a sure sign of an empty soultank!)

Remember, if you are running on empty, YOU are the only one who can plan soul moments and fill up. No one else is in charge of making that happen. It is your responsibility to make sure you are living a happy, fulfilling, and passion-filled life.

Let me be clear:
Ignoring the signs, skipping this step, or avoiding taking care of yourself are NOT options.

#MoxieMemo: Making time for everyone except YOU is not selfless... *It is selfish.*

When you are your best self you are able to serve others with a passionate soul.

Instead of being overwhelmed that no one can help you, I encourage you to flip that feeling and say this to yourself instead:

I AM IN CONTROL OF HOW FULL MY SOULTANK IS!

How exciting! No one can take this away from me.

So, are you ready? It's time to put your Soultank List together

Pour yourself a cup of coffee or tea, a glass of wine, or whatever beverage inspires you to get creative!

Fire Up Step 1: Idea Storming Soul Session

1. What activities FIRE YOU UP and fill your soultank?

2. What makes you smile, relax, laugh, sing, shout or dance uncontrollably?

3. What PASSION CULTURE do you want to inspire in your life or in your business?

4. Do you have a charity you love to serve, support, and promote?

5. What do you have a divine passion for, in this season? Write these things down.
   (i.e. wine, yoga, dogs, cats, golf, hiking, travel, gardening)

6. List out your hobbies:
   (Maybe you collect vintage vehicles, vinyl records, or typewriters, or _____)

If you aren't sure WHAT you are passionate about or how to define it, no worries - that is why we are doing this together now.

It's never too late to design a SOULTANK MENU, so let's get started!

Fire Up Step 2: Fill Your Soultank List

The goal here is to write a list of 11+ things that fill your soultank, make you laugh, and generally FIRE YOU UP!

1.

2.

3.

4.

5.

6.

7.

8.

9.

10.

11.

Remember, you can download a full version of the exercises in the book by going here: debratrappen.com/fireupworkbook

Remember, the items on your list should be things you are or can do right now. They can be free activities, types of conversations, things you love to create, etc. The thought of them brings a smile to your face and ignites a spark inside.

Your passions are those things or activities that FIRE YOU UP and fuel your soultank!

Fire It Up To 11:
Have some FUN with your list and create a Pinterest pin board that represents your passion list. When you are feeling like you could use a mindset shift – you can visit your board for a quick attitude BOOST!

Fire Up Step 3: Infuse Your Passions

Once you have defined your soultank list it is time to INFUSE those things into your daily life.

Take some time each week to schedule in your SOULTANK time... you can always squeeze in a 2-minute-puppy-belly-rubbing-session or a fun, fierce, focused 30-second dance party on those days when you just don't "have time"!

The people in your life will thank you for taking the time, and so will your soul.

Can't imagine having success scheduling ME TIME with consistency?

Try partnering up with a friend and keeping each other accountable. It takes around 21 days to rewire neural pathways and begin building a new way of thinking about your values and 42 days (another two sets of 21 days, for a total of 63 days) to establish a new habit and way of thinking.

Give yourself grace and set yourself up for success.

Fire It Up To 11:
Create a recurring monthly or quarterly reminder to revisit your list. Add in new passions and remove those you are no longer interested in pursuing. A fresh, ever-changing list (or pin board) is an ACTIVE one!

Fire Up Step 4: Design Soulful Experiences

Let's take a quick look at how we can use our soultank list in our life and business to create soulful, memorable experiences for our clients and connections.

Fire Up Story:

Sofia Bennett is a small business owner who has a passion for wine and loves to host events.

During our sessions together, we put together a plan to infuse wine into her business and attract clients who share a similar passion. We reviewed these areas:

Where could she host her next client event?
- A local winery for a wine tasting event.

What could her client appreciation gifts be?
- A customized bottle of her favorite wine or personal blend she created.

Where could she network to meet new clients?
- Winery or wine bar events: vertical wine tastings, live music, cheese pairings or one of those fun "wine & painting" events.

Many of these are also in alignment with her values of creativity, knowledge, relationships and adventure.

Are you starting to see the importance of having your values and passions defined and infused into your life plan?

Fire Up Story:

Let's continue Tina Mitchell's story...

While Tina was writing out her soultank list, she realized she was going to need more than the list to really infuse these elements into her daily life. She decided to design a 30-day challenge to help her stay on track and connected with her soultank list.

She named it "The Reflection Challenge" because it is a balance of doing things for her and doing things for others. She uses it as a tool to enrich her life and the lives of others around her, while allowing her to work ON her life not just IN it!

Tina shares, "I also really wanted my values and "purpose" to show through, which is **inspiring others to live their dream**. This is why I added in creating positive triggers to help them identify and overcome moments that may distract them from their dreams!

Want to join? Visit: reflectionchallenge.com

Have you started to dream up ways you can put your first two lists together to FIRE UP your life and business?

I would love to know what you are cooking up... tweet me @debra11 and use #FireMeUp11!

Making time for everyone
except you is not *selfless...*
It is selfish.

When you are your
best self you are able
to serve others with a
passionate, joyful **soul.**

DEBRATRAPPEN.COM

Chapter 3
Uncover Your Purpose

"Be yourself; everyone else is taken!"
—Oscar Wilde

Your purpose is constantly empowering you.

Your life's purpose is something you do so effortlessly and naturally, you have probably overlooked it for many years.

It is likely inspiring you to learn and grow.

Your purpose is so simple that it fires you up and into your magnificence when are on the right path. You can feel it when you find it.

It feels right.

I have had countless conversations with friends, clients, and Fire Up! community members about defining their "PURPOSE".

- Some people have a foggy idea of what theirs is
- Some have NO idea what it is
- Others are so overwhelmed by the concept of UNCOVERING THEIR PURPOSE that they shrink back and hide from the process
- Most of the time – people are getting their purpose confused with their motivations (aka Values)

Let's start digging in and defining the term PURPOSE.

Your purpose is what I love to call your Tribal Talent – a special skill/gifting/talent YOU bring to the table that your village, squad, team, tribe, family, etc. seeks from YOU – ALL THE TIME!

To you, your talent comes so naturally to you that everyone must have it, so it really isn't that special.

Your "purpose" or skill is NOT unique, but how you do it and where you focus it – IS UNIQUE TO YOU!

This is usually the mind bender for many. There is this misconception that we are the only person who has our purpose. We look to Mother Theresa, Ellen, or Oprah… and think our purpose should look like theirs in size, shape, and vision. I am here to tell you – YOU can be the Oprah or Ellen of YOUR tribe!

Just because these women educate, entertain, and elevate their mega audiences, does not preclude you from doing the same with YOUR audience – regardless if it is 10 people or 10,000+. What makes your purpose unique is your own sizzle, style, and the people you serve!

Every tribe needs a Amy Schumer, Ina Garten, Madeleine Albright, Oprah, Joel Osteen, Christine Caine, Brene Brown, and so on...

Now, let me share an example of how PURPOSE, WHY, AND VALUES can be confused:

I work quite a bit with GenX'ers who are starting their own businesses, getting ready to reenter the workforce, or trying to figure out WHAT IS NEXT! Some are raising small children. Some are raising tweens. Some are already empty nesters.

When we start the "purpose" conversations, most of them cringe. Many feel guilty or shameful for "being this age" and not knowing what it is.

(Shame off you, if this is you, too!)

Many automatically claim their CHILDREN are their purpose. Regardless if they are women who have been blessed to raise their children 24/7 and call themselves SAHM's, Chief Home Operator, Queen Of The Castle, or (fill in the blank) OR if they are killing it in Corporate America or as a business owner to bring home the bacon...

This is where I put on the breaks. I say this - with love: your children are not your **purpose!**

Your purpose is not directly connected to another SPECIFIC person.

Children are a divine gift, a significant responsibility, and a magnificent motivation - but they are NOT your **_purpose_** on the planet.

Take a moment and think about it this way:

Do you believe that your purpose did not begin until you had children or that it will abruptly end when they move out of the house?

This is why I believe so many parents (mostly Mama Bears) deal with such depression when their children move out and start lives of their own. It WOULD BE depressing if you thought your life's purpose was over when that happened!

Rejoice in the fact that your purpose is still fully intact when your little ones walk out the door.

The amazing news is that being a parent allows you to tap into your purpose – in some way, shape or form. When you define your purpose you will start to see it in your interactions with your children, spouse, friends, family, colleagues, and beyond. Those are moments to celebrate!

To give some clarity to this, here are some examples of simple "PURPOSE DECLARATIONS" from past clients:

- I am the peacemaker.
- I entertain people.
- I listen to and comfort people.
- I connect people and opportunities.
- I inspire others to live their dream now.
- I teach people to organize.
- I solve problems.
- I gather people together to serve.
- I encourage people to live intentionally.
- I speak the truth with grace and love.

You get the idea and can definitely see why many parents get their purpose confused with parenting. Parenting taps into ALL of these talents

It is also important to realize that the journey doesn't end once your define your purpose. Conscious living actually begins at that moment. You will be working to live by and engage it personally and professionally every day.

Are you ready?

I believe your purpose can be stated in 11 words or less.

To get you rolling, and hopefully inspire you, let me share my purpose, as well as my personal purpose statement.

My purpose: **I FIRE PEOPLE UP.**

Sure, you could also say: I get people "unstuck", help people find clarity in chaos, shift and ignite their mindset, inspire them to take things to an 11 with many ideas and straight-talk... but the end result of all of these is feeling **FIRED UP.**

My personal fire up statement adds a little sass and moxie and makes it my own:

"To ignite passion, infuse purpose, and inspire progress by connecting, engaging, elevating and empowering the magnificent connections and brilliant ideas in my world."

I wrote this in 2002. Every single time I read this it fires ME up. Yours should too.

Let's get going on defining your PURPOSE.

Fire Up Step 1: Listen

Why? People are likely already telling you your purpose!

"Thank you! You are so good at (fill in the blank)!

The blanks might be:

- Teaching me something new when I see you
- Comforting me in my time of need
- Telling me what I need to hear, whether I like it or not
- Making me laugh and reminding me to have fun...

What do you think yours is?
(Write the first thing that comes to mind!)

Fire Up Step 2: Uncover Your Purpose

I encourage you to slow down to respect and honor the process of discovering your purpose. Schedule time when you can unwind. Pour yourself a cup of coffee, tea, or a velvety glass of wine, find a quiet spot and explore your purpose

To get you started, here are some questions:

1. These people inspire me:

2. What conversations set my soul on fire?

3. What activities do I get lost in where I lose track of time?

4. What do people ask me to help them with?

5. If I could only share/teach one message to one group of people... what would my message be and whom would those people be?

6. If I knew I would never fail, what would I do, be or have?

Remember don't rush through this process. However, don't spend too much time laboring over each step either.

Trust yourself.

Write down the answers that immediately come to mind. There is no magic pill formula to define your purpose. You have creative freedom, flexibility, and time to write, revise, and refine it... as long as it takes to get you there.

Remember, you can download a full version of the exercises in the book by going here: debratrappen.com/fireupworkbook

Remember, our lives are designed to be overflowing with lessons and challenges. When you find yourself stuck on a question or exercise, try focusing on what answers ARE clear. Revel in those successes. Celebrate the clarity in those moments. Discovery will come if you are willing to push through and take your tenacious spirit to an 11!

Fire Up Story:

Meet April Briggs. April is a creative.

She loves using her creativity to inspire people - whether they are in her chair getting their hair done or at her dining room table being fed. She is passionate about cooking and loves getting people to try food they say they don't like. As a mother of FIVE children she is always on the go, so she loves to listen to podcasts and video messages while she is driving. (Obviously she doesn't WATCH the video while she is driving - she only listens!) Sometimes her children are in the car and the messages/words spoken MATTER on many levels in many lives.

Her purpose is to GATHER and SHEPHERD PEOPLE.

April's story will show you the power of designing, defining and leveraging your values, soultank, and purpose.   Here we go:

2016 was a tornado of a year. I lost my footing - physically and emotionally. Toward the end of year, I began to find myself and my path again. The lessons of the year changed me - forever.

In the process of getting back on my feet, I began refining my personal values. Among a few other values, wholeheartedness is one I wanted to deeply focus on this year.

I realized in my quest to be wholehearted there was a need to slow down and create a margin in my life for my Faith and God's presence in my life. Not in a 'rushed, gotta fit it in where I can' way, but in a very focused, intentional way.

I set out to listen to a faith-based leadership or empowering message/podcast every single day. Monday through Friday I was going to resource myself.

As I was doing this, I had theses thoughts: "I am a mother of FIVE. My children are a bit older now and man I sure could have used this when my children were little! I know there are ladies out there who are so busy that it would be so great if I could send this to them every day. Kind of like cooking up a good meal for a friend in need and then serving it to them!" (April LOVES to make food analogies, too!)

I talked with a couple of my girlfriends and asked them if they would like to join me in a daily devotional message. The plan was we would all listen and then share what resonated with each other via text messages. We could also share prayer requests in our circles and be truly ON PURPOSE about growing together and growing with God.

Not only is this changing my life by filling my soul tank with SOUL FOOD, it is also impacting the lives of my community. I am so excited to see where this leads..."

Want to connect with April? You can find her sharing her story of transformation on Facebook: facebook.com/metamorphis4

Are you starting to see your purpose in reveal itself?

Don't worry if you are having a hard time "seeing" your purpose in your every day activities, job, or feel like it is disconnected from current roles and responsibilities. Sometimes it shows up in and fill the most unexpected moments – like April's story.

Oh, and before you go for a full "reinvention", stop and go thru this next exercise. It will help you take a look at what you are doing now and **FIND THE WINS!**

Ask yourself these three questions:

1. Which values are honored in my current roles?

2. When is my soultank being filled in these roles?

3. How is my purpose being leveraged and honed?

Even if you eventually decide you are not in the ideal industry or job, you may be able to find greater fulfillment through how you do what you do right now, experience more joy in and from it, and pour your greatness into your world as you look for your next step!

Finding the WINS in your current season is so incredibly important. Don't skip this step! You may not even realize how close you are to authentically living out loud.

Ultimately, living your life with focused intention and embracing your PURPOSE will allow you to truly focus on things that matter most. So, please don't give up. Push through the moments of frustration during this process of discovery.

You are worth it.

Living your life with

*intention and
embracing your purpose*

will allow you to truly
focus on things that
matter most!

Chapter 4
Create Your Niche

"Be who you are and say what you feel, because those who mind don't matter and those who matter don't mind." – Dr. Seuss

The final Core Four element is all about discovering and formulating YOUR niche then SHARING it with people! **This step leverages the first three elements – values, passions, and purpose.**

This process will help you define who **YOUR IDEAL CLIENT** is... notice I did not say your ONLY client.

The reality is, too many independent sales professionals and solopreneurs start out believing they can or should be **all things to all people**. They believe they are "leaving business on the table" when they focus on a target market.

However, businesses owners taking on this EVERYTHING attitude risk many issues including burnout, exhaustion, confusion, and failure. By defining a specific **niche** (a well-defined segment of a larger market), you know what message/experience to deliver; your customers know exactly what to expect; and your sphere of champions knows how to share your message with others!

Being all things to all people is impossible, so you must craft niches to complement your personality, your business, and your resources. Creating your niche will give your business the greatest chance of success, but where do you start?

Simply put —> DEFINE IT.

Here are 5 steps to get you on the path to defining your niche:

Fire Up Step 1: Pick An Industry To Serve
Start by asking yourself some questions to help you choose:

1. What industries or products do you know?
2. What industries or products do you love?

3. What industries do you have influence in?

Is there one industry that is the answer to all three questions? If so, start there!

Remember, it is important to have a passion for what you do AND for those you serve. As an entrepreneur, you get to choose – so choose wisely. You might know a ton about the wine industry and you may have influence in it, but if you don't get up every single day with an electric attitude to make, taste, and sell more wine...

Well, you get the idea!

Fire Up Step 2: Define Your Ideal Customer

Get focused... this is who you are going to work with every day. What type of lifestyle does your target audience live? How old are they? What are they passionate about doing, solving, or being?

Rather than choosing a broad category, narrow your target customer down, think about things like: gender, geographical location, married or single, hobbies, employer or occupation, etc.

When you define your ideal customer you are also defining the language you use, pin pointing the platforms you use to engage and promote on, and allowing yourself to focus in and learn all you can about that specific demographic.

BONUS: All of these help in strengthening your brand as "The GO TO" in the niche.

Fire Up Step 3: Specialize

Many small businesses make a big mistake here, and try to offer every type of service or product they can for their market. Remember, the concept is being known for a specialty. For instance, saying "I sell real estate in Seattle" is just too broad. "I sell bungalows (or condos or multi-unit buildings) in the Capitol Hill area" is specific. When you state your specialty, people are able to catalogue it and can refer you business much easier.

Fire Up Step 4: Look For Under-Served Audiences

There are always groups of people who have specific conditions or needs that automatically make it difficult to find service providers. Maybe a "generalization" has caused your competitors to label a specific generation "not interesting yet". When this group finds out THEY are your specialty, you will have secured clients for life. If you market well and provide them a platform to share the story of your business, they will also help you build your business with referrals.

Fire Up Step 5: Be In The Know

There are many ways to find out trends in your niche of choice. Get rolling with these:

- **Do a search online.** If you want to start a *personal trainer* or *life coach* company, do a quick online search to find out how many others are in this space in your area. This quick snapshot will teach you a lot about the industry you are interested in, how others are marketing themselves, and possibly even show a gap in the space.

- **Set up an RSS Feed** to keep up on top industry blogs and bloggers.

- **Put together a list of key hashtags to follow.** Look over the first four keys and pull out key words to use.

  For instance, if you want to focus on LUXURY CLIENTS – think about what they are also buying, where they are spending time, and who also serves them. Some key hashtags may be: #luxury #travel #golf #wine #theatre #investing

- **PARTICIPATE** on social media platforms.
  Join a Facebook or LinkedIn Group where these ideal clients will be.
  Set up lists on Twitter to keep in touch with what your ideal clients and those who also serve them are up to!

Last, but not least:
LET'S FORMULATE YOUR NICHE STATEMENT!

An ideal niche statement formula looks like this:
ideal client + problem + solution + sizzle = success

Begin by writing down these four elements:

1. **Your ideal client/audience**
   Who do you want to work with every day?

2. **Their problem**
   What is their biggest problem YOU want to solve every single day?

3. **Your solution**
   How will you solve their biggest problem?

4. **Your sizzle**
   How do you want people to feel when they work with you?

This can be a trying process. Sometimes it helps to see what other people have created for their businesses.

Here are some examples to get you on the right track:

"I serve growth driven business professionals with a deep desire to evolve, learn, grow, and succeed at the highest level.

My mission is to help these high achievers design a strategic and profitable online business and marketing plan. I'm there to break down barriers, help them get unstuck, and overcome mental or financial blocks that will increase their creativity, income, and results."

~ Rebekah Radice, rebekahradice.com

I am looking for women that want to start a blog or have started a blog and wonder, "What do I do next? What do I do after I start my blog?"

The women bloggers struggle with getting more blog traffic, getting engagement on their posts, and making money from blogging. They are working hard, but not really seeing a lot of results on their blogs.

I help women through personal coaching and my signature program, Find Your Tribe Online. I show them how to find their people online and bring them back to their blogs. I give them a plan to follow to help them avoid getting overwhelmed and stuck in "shiny object syndrome."

When women bloggers work with me I want them to feel encouraged that anything is possible with their blogs! I want them to feel a sense of calm and peace when I come on the scene and help them.

Jennifer Snyder, womenwinningonline.com

Here is an example of how I worked it all into a fun bio write up:

I am an Empowerment Coach, Speaker, and Author (aka the Chief of Sass and Moxie).

My purpose is to fire people up! My mission is igniting the bold women of GenX. I guide them to define and design the best version of themselves, uncover who they are meant to serve, and declare what success means to them. Ultimately equipping them to intentionally live their signature life out loud, serve their communities, and become the change they wish to see - with focus, confidence, and purpose.

When I'm not idea-storming my next adventure or writing, interviewing, or recording in my Fire Up! studio or enjoying quiet time with God, you will find me walking my pups, devouring books and podcasts, watching Sci-Fi flicks, taking photos, or traveling and wine tasting with my hubby and besties across the globe!

~ Debra Trappen, debratrappen.com

Are you ready to set your business and career up for success?

If you are shouting out YES, your next step is to work through the 5 keys in this chapter and create your niche statement.

This will help you get clarity.

Now it is time to boldly go out there, get the attention of your target audience and ROCK YOUR VISION!

Remember, you can download a full version of the exercises in the book by going here:
debratrappen.com/fireupworkbook

When you are *authentic*
it allows others in
and *attracts* people and
opportunities to you
like a magnet!

DEBRATRAPPEN.COM

Chapter 5
Embracing Your Signature Self

"Imperfection is beauty, madness is genius, and it is better to be absolutely ridiculous than absolutely boring." - Marilyn Monroe

Now that you have your Core Four defined and a strong personal brand foundation and message to share, it is time get comfortable in this new skin... REALLY comfortable.

Are you ready?

Let's start with the basics of infusing your Core Four while being your signature self – both online and offline.

You know the world is full of knock-offs, spinoffs, and cheap imitations. You realize being "genuine" seems all to often to be the exception, not the norm. You know there is only ONE person just like you, so why do you fight being "yourself"?

I believe it all starts with LOVING yourself. Which leads me to the first tip.

Fire Up Tip 1: Stop The Negative Self-Talk

Take a moment and think about how you are talking to yourself. Are you being kind or inflicting shame on yourself?

You speak encouraging words to and believe in the greatness of others in your life. Where is the grace for yourself in all of this?

What makes you and me always want to "be (or compare ourselves to) someone else"?

Well, for one, you likely don't "talk to yourself" like you talk to friends. You can be downright MEAN to yourself - calling yourself stupid, fat, ugly - not worthy. With all of those adjectives floating around your head – it is no wonder you don't embrace, elevate or empower yourself. You can understand how this would seriously get in the way of a healthy personal brand foundation!

Want to combat this?

Pretend you are talking to your 7-year-old self!

Would you say those things to her/him? I didn't think so. Whenever you are formulating "negative self talk" in your mind – stop and picture yourself with those piggy tails or in those Wonder Woman or Spiderman Underoos that made you feel like you could conquer the world. Now try saying those negative words to your mini you. It is crazy how well this works!

Enough is enough. It is time to acknowledge your greatness, embrace your distinctive combination of values, passions, and purpose, and get excited that you really do have **your own path**.

Start believing there isn't anyone like you. Accept your responsibility to be the best version of **YOU** as possible!

What do you have to be afraid of?

Why do you hold on to these negative thoughts and consistently put yourself down?

Could it be you are worried that:
- Your relationships might improve?
- Your businesses will flourish?

- Your consistent, day-to-day emotion could be HAPPINESS?

I know, it sounds CRAZY when you read those statements out loud, but this is exactly what you are doing.

Come on now. You know deep down you deserve happiness, love, and success.

REPEAT THIS AFTER ME:
I deserve happiness, love, and success.

(Go on, I will wait.)

Now, SAY IT AGAIN. This time, stand up, put your hands in the air, and SHOUT IT OUT.

I deserve happiness, love, and success.

If you didn't try shouting it out while standing up "with your hands in the air like you just don't care" - you only cheated yourself.

The rest of us have HUGE smiles on our faces!

Now, embrace this:
The world needs to be blessed by your talents - YOUR special gifts.

For this all to happen, you have to get over your negative thoughts, believe in yourself and start sharing your best self with the world!

Want or need some help?

Here are 11 Affirmations to start infusing into your self-talk time:

1. Loving myself is fabulously essential to my happiness and positive attitude.
2. I deserve to passionately go after my goals and do what makes my soul sizzle.
3. Accepting myself unconditionally gives me the power to succeed and rock my purpose.
4. I am an amazing person who deserves happiness, success, and love.
5. I accept myself deeply and completely.
6. I have limitless confidence in my talents and abilities.
7. Others will be inspired by my courage to be myself.
8. I will take time to recognize and celebrate my achievements.
9. I look forward to discovering new layers of myself every single day.
10. There is no one like me and I can't wait to share my talents today.
11. I am divine, complete and totally equipped to live my life and purpose out loud!

Now it is your turn.   Write your own 11 Affirmations. Use my list to inspire you and be sure to add YOUR own signature sass to each statement. You want these statements to fire you up and fill you with JOY!

1.

2.

3.

4.

5.

6.

7.

8.

9.

10.

11.

Fire Up Tip 2: DEFINE Your Own Success

Take a moment and ask yourself:
Do I know what SUCCESS means to me?
What does it look like TODAY?
What it will LOOK like tomorrow?
How does it make me FEEL?

Let's review a couple of key reasons defining your own success" is a process worthy of your attention:

1: If you don't define what it means to you, the definitions the world sets will become yours.

Most organizations praise sales numbers, award top producers, and reward achievement with and around

MONEY. The amount of money you make can't be the only way you define victory.

If you are not careful and focused on your own definition of success, the media's idea of the perfect body, a praise-worthy title or position, etc. will become yours...

2: You are able to truly support other's successes without feeling less than or in competition with them!

When you are fuzzy about your own, everyone else's achievements starts to look like it "might be" or "should be" YOURS, not theirs!

Here a couple of examples of success statements from two Fire Up! community members:

"I will feel successful when I am able to be home when my children get home from school, make them a healthy dinner, and tuck them in every night."

"I will feel successful when I am able to send my parents on a vacation every year with my business that allows me to work anywhere in the world – anytime!"

You can build a wonderful life around EITHER of these success statements – running the same type of business!

Yes, these two versions of success LOOK very different, however, BOTH of these women are marketing experts who serve small businesses. One focuses on local businesses and the other works with companies all over the globe.

The woman who wants to be home every night USED TO be consumed by thoughts of inadequacy when she would see others in her field speaking on stages across the globe. Now she sees that the lifestyle of traveling would NOT make her feel successful – in fact, it would make her feel like she was missing out on what was important TO HER!

So, now that you have a couple of key reasons WHY this is so important, here is a simple exercise to get you rolling. Start by completing these sentences:

I am successful when _____

_____

_____.

I am successful when _____

_____

_____.

I am successful when _____

_____

_____.

I will feel successful when _____

_____

_____.

I will feel successful when _____

_____

_____.

I will feel successful when _____

_____

_____.

**Feel free to create as many of
these as you would like!**

Now that you have defined what YOUR SUCCESS looks like, take time every day to review where you were able to honor these statements.

These custom statements will make it easier to see it, celebrate it and truly revel in it!

Fire Up Tip 3: Stop Comparing Yourself To Other People

Battling or embracing your self-doubt and focusing on "the competition" are some of the top ways we keep ourselves from achieving GREATNESS.

If you are waging war against yourself, STOP.

Remember, there is NO ONE like you. You are in competition with no one. Reset your mind and focus on your passions, your purpose, your values... those things that make you uniquely YOU.

Shine your distinctive self every day...
Spread your spirited sparkle...
Sprinkle your feisty glitter...

Being your SIGNATURE SELF is your responsibility.
No one else can do it for you.

REMEMBER: Focusing on what everyone else is doing is only keeping YOU from your greatness. It doesn't slow them down one bit...

When you feel yourself slipping into comparison mode – revisit your SUCCESS statements and find joy there!

Fire Up Tip 4: Write A List Of Mindset Shift Activities To Help You Win These Battles

1. Call a friend.

The REAL one who doesn't whisper fluffy kitten talk in your ear, but gives it to you STRAIGHT, kicks you in the toosh when you need it, and reminds you of your greatness. Who are YOUR go to people?

MY GO TO CALL LIST:

1.

2.

3.

4.

5.

2. Take a walk.

Leave your phone at home. Enjoy the fresh air and reconnect with the life sounds around you. If you have a dog, bring him/her along. Dogs are fabulous companions and have been known to listen (and solve) many problems.

3. Indulge in ME TIME.

Try this: Close the curtains. Light some candles. Slip into a bubble bath – in the middle of the day. Yep. INDULGE. Don't judge. Try it. It works. *Not into bubble baths – substitute your own "me time" activity!*

4. Fly your freak flag.

Crank the music up and have a personal dance party. Pity parties are just plain lame.

Dance parties fill your soultank.

5. Kick into an SMP Session!

A what?? A **S**tretch, **M**editate, and **P**rayer Session!

I find that when I slow down, stretch, and get back to my true center - I return with a divinely unstoppable attitude. There is something magical and renewing when we invest time in ourselves.

Take a moment and write down what YOU do to renew and refocus your mind when those irritating self-doubt thoughts start whispering in your ear. Be specific so when you need a reset it's easy to do!

Need help? Take a look at your soultank list and add a few of those!

MY MINDSET SHIFT LIST:

1.

2.

3.

4.

5.

6.

7.

8.

9.

10.

11.

Feeling bold and daring? Share them with me on Twitter using the hashtag #FireMeUp11 and tag me @debra11.

You have invested precious time into designing a solid personal brand foundation. It is your turn to knock out self-doubt and embrace your brilliant, signature self!

Now, I'm going to get on my fiery redhead soapbox to recap, so put your seatbelt on, my darling!

YOU were born an original.
Don't live like a copy.
Find your voice and use it.
Embrace your uniqueness.
YOU are here for a purpose.
Stop focusing on what others are doing.
It is a waste of your time.
Get comfortable in your skin.
Be intentional with your choice to be your
BEST YOU every day.
Sparkle. Shine. Inspire.
B-R-E-A-T-H-E and SMILE!

You are born an original.
Don't live like a copy.
Find your voice.
Embrace your uniqueness.

Sparkle. Shine.
Inspire.

DEBRATRAPPEN.COM

Chapter 6
Sharing Your Story

"The most powerful person in the world is the story teller. The storyteller sets the vision, values and agenda of an entire generation that is to come." - Steve Jobs

Now that you have your Core Four elements defined and a healthy attitude adjustment on embracing your magnificence - your story is ready for the "unveiling party" online!

A strong personal foundation and brand (like yours!) weaves and tells a powerful, memorable, and believable story.

Stories inspire.

When you are able to INSPIRE your audience you are, in essence, sharing and selling yourself at the same time. You effortlessly attract ideal connections when you live your vision, values, and passions out loud. When you LIVE and SHARE your signature brand story. Let's talk about some of the top tips to leverage and share your Core Four story online:

Fire Up Tip 1: Visual Storytelling

One of the simplest ways to share your Core Four online is by visually telling your story. Using photos and videos, also increases your engagement – especially over plain text posts.

It is time to pull out your values and passions list WORDS and put them into action online. While sharing your love of hiking, wine, dogs, or yoga can be easily shared with a few words in a status update – adding some sizzle to your content with a photo or video takes it to an 11!

The more detailed, engaging, and consistent your story is – the more memorable it is!

Need some inspiration or examples?

Here are a couple of my clients:

> **Liz** is incredibly passionate about volunteering in her community. She regularly would post

updates like "I am off to volunteer at a local shelter today!" Now, there is nothing wrong with the post. However, when she switched over to sharing photos from the exciting shelter project she was managing, her engagement increased tenfold!

Why? Quite simply: she was sharing the story – her behind the scenes – with her friends and followers. They could SEE it and connect with it... and were inspired to ask questions about the work she was doing. A few people even got involved with her project!

Susie is a passionate foodie, however her career has nothing to do with either... or does it? Susie is a real estate professional. That means she serves and sells her community – a town filled with fabulous restaurants and a personal gourmet kitchen packed with cookbooks and homemade nibbles.

She was not sure how to share this in a relevant way, so we put together a simple strategy for her.

Instead of posting she is "cooking/baking today or perusing cookbooks" she now takes a photo of the delicious food she makes and shares it on Facebook. The engagement grows with each post. Not only is she sharing her personal passion for food and cooking – she is creating a deeper connection with other foodies and attracting new connections that are interested too!

Fire Up Tip 2: Blog. Vlog. Podcast. Oh My!

Part of sharing your personal brand story is about engaging and attracting your ideal connections. In addition, the ability to influence and impact your world increases exponentially. In order to be recognized as a thought-leader or inspiration in your industry you must leverage your Core Four and **SHARE YOUR THOUGHTS**.

Sounds simple, however so many people get caught up in excuses and never make it to the sharing piece.

BLOGGING:

You don't have to write a book to share your thoughts. Start with writing a blog post on your own website – once a week or even once/twice a month. If you don't have your own website, offer to guest post on a website that focuses on serving your niche or industry.

Weekly/monthly contributions introduce who you are to the world, they also show tenacity, consistency and that you are literate. If you don't have the time for writing in this current season of your life, there are options.

A few of my clients have hired a trusted professional to write for them - in THEIR VOICE. There are ghostwriters who will take the time to get to know you, your style, and will provide custom posts for you. No more "canned" excuses. Take action and get it done! Remember, good, error-free content that shares you and shines a light on your brand is what you are seeking.

Another easy way to share your thoughts is to curate excellent content from other authors that speak to your Core Four. What blogs are you already reading? If you are not following any blogs now, do a little research and start following the bloggers who resonate with you. Sign up to receive new posts in your inbox and/or follow them on Twitter. When their post evokes an emotion from you – share a link to it on your blog, as well as your social media platforms.

The key is to ADD YOUR OWN THOUGHTS when you share it. Let other people know what you liked, what riled you up, or what you are going to try because of it.

Don't let perfection stand in the way of promoting your brand and sharing your story!

VLOGGING:

If you enjoy being in front of the camera, start a video blog. These do not have to be professional video quality! Use your laptop camera, a couple of well-placed lamps, and a quality external microphone to get started. You can be the solo star of your show sharing your perspectives, passions and purpose; you can interview others who service your niche/industry; or a fun combination of both.

PODCAST:

If you don't want to be on camera, but still have something to say, start a podcast. There are plenty of great resources out there to get you started. Pop on over to Google and search "How do I start a podcast?"

Fire Up Story:

A dear friend and business collaborator, Marguerite Crespillo, brilliantly weaves together her values and fuels her soultank with a passion project! She clearly values **building and nurturing relationships and making a difference**; and she is passionate about **sharing her knowledge**.

In 2014, Marguerite realized how frustrated she was with the lack of real content and information in the real estate industry and had so much she wanted to share, so she decided to start her own podcast. The "Real Estate, Real World" show is packed with conversations highlighting people who are serving and doing the REAL work in the space.

She has produced over 80 episodes and the show is not only growing in viewership, the journey has been a blast. Marguerite enjoys sharing her perspectives and helping provide simple solutions to the day-to-day struggles her audience experiences in an ever-changing industry. The cherry on top is being able to introduce her listeners to brilliant minds and concepts that will help them grow their businesses and give them control of the most important asset they possess - TIME! Learn more: margueritecrespillo.com

Have an idea for a podcast and not sure how to implement? Tweet me @debra11 and tag #FireMeUp11!

Fire Up Tip 3: Host Events

A FUN way to share your Core Four is putting together events that support and represent them! If you are passionate about dogs and wine – put together (or participate in) a walk-a-thon to raise funds for a local animal shelter - and add a tent for tasting local wines at the finish line!

Fire Up Story:

One of my dearest clients and friends, Carol Farrar of 1850 Realty, NAILS this concept with her Throwback Thursday events.

Carol values and has a true passion for infusing her 3 C's: community, collaboration and contribution. However, she wasn't sure how to put all of the pieces of the puzzle together. During one of our d11 #FireMeUp11 Sessions the two of us put together a strategic plan to infuse all of her C's and "Throwback Thursdays" were born! #TBT is monthly event that supports a local brewery (infusing her background in and love for craft beer) and brings awareness to a local charity while "throwing one back" with the local community. People love it!

These monthly events fulfill her 3 C's, are highly attended, and have produced more recognition, for Carol and her team, as supporters of the community. It differentiates 1850 Realty from others in the San Diego area, attracts attention from others in the real estate industry, AND she is having fun doing it!

Planning events and sparking conversations connected to your Core Four will not only be interesting to plan, host and continue; it will let your friends and followers know a bit more about you with each event and promotion.

Keeping your story content authentic and interesting makes it easier for clients to delight in the experience of following you, reading and sharing your posts, remembering key points, and sparking actions that builds deeper relationships and more business!

Fire Up Tip 4: Start A Business or Side-Hustle

I am often asked "How do you turn your passion into your career?" This is a sticky question because not EVERYONE has the ability to do that or a passion that translates into a solid business idea. However, it DOES happen. Your story may be the perfect way to promote a passion project that is an additional revenue stream. The best way to walk through this is to share another example.

Fire Up Story:

Meet Rachel. She is the CEO and founder of The Rachel Adams Group.

Rachel values a healthy lifestyle and mentoring, and is passionate about seeing the positive affects her experiences and wisdom brings to other's lives. Now, while real estate is in her blood and is a wonderful career, she finds great joy in encouraging others to lead their best life.

Rachel's love for inspiring others, combined with her own unique and powerful journey to health and happiness, led her to co-create the **Lost to Found 90 Days Book and Program.** Woven into the course are the ability to track your food/water/workouts, write in your online journal, update your progress pics, receive clean eating tips and meal plans, as well as video shorts with exercise tips.

When you visit the website, her STORY is front and center. You hear the WHY (motivation) behind the program and it is very personal and vulnerable.

You can FEEL how much she truly believes your potential is unlimited and her program is a beautiful representation of her values and passions coming together in a life lived out loud!

Get to know Rachel and learn about the program here: lost2found90.com

Are you starting to you see how your story, whether it was the struggle, the journey, or the victory, would inspire someone to purchase your program, products or services?

Need help idea storming and activating?
Tweet me @debra11 and let's talk it out.

Effortlessly attract
ideal connections when
you live your
vision, values, and passions
out loud.
What's your *signature*
brand story?

Chapter 7
Leveraging Social Media

"Good content isn't about good storytelling.
It's about telling a true story well." - Ann Handley

Now that you have fashioned your story and decided what format want to share it in – it's time to shine a light and decide WHERE to share your journey. When you courageously share you create a spark that ignites and INSPIRES others to be brave. Maybe you will inspire them to make a decision, do what they always dreamed of, or (ideally) work with you! I often get the question, "Where should I post online? There are so many social media platforms out there, how do I know which one is best for me?"

The answer is in YOUR Core Four.

There are digital marketing platforms that will tickle your fancy and one or two that will fit you better than the others! Here are some steps to help you figure out which one you should try out first!

Fire Up Step 1: Clarify Your Goals

The first thing you want to do is figure out what your top reasons for being online personally and professionally are.

Start by asking yourself these questions:

1. Do I need to increase my visibility with a certain industry or influence group? If so, where?

2. Do I want to build credibility on a current passion or in a current or new industry? If so, what?

3. Am I seeking to secure new clients? If so, who are they?

4. Do I want to build a community based on my soultank interests and passions? If so, what interest/passion?

5. Am I looking to uncover new business opportunities? If so, what?

6. Am I ready for a career move or niche change? If so, what does that look like?

Fire Up Step 2: Know The Platforms

This step reviews some key platforms and tips and tricks on these elements by breaking them down.

- What is it? (A brief description of the platform)
- Ideas on what to share
- Who should you connect with there
- Who to connect with and why

FACEBOOK PROFILE

What is it? An online platform to stay connected with friends and family, to discover what's going on in the world, and to share and express what matters to you. Ideas on what to share: The moments of your life – mostly personal sprinkled with some professional. Photos, videos, blog posts, and quotes are the most frequent posts. Visuals tend to get much higher engagement.

Who should you connect with? People you know, like and trust. If you want to connect with people you don't know well, be sure to utilize the "list" option they offer. You can choose what those people see, as you wish.

FACEBOOK PAGE

What is it? A business page you can share your business information on as often as you want. If you are an entrepreneur who owns a small service company, like a consulting firm, real estate business, or likewise – a page allows you to share your business with those who want to know about it. You should periodically invite your "friends" to come over and like your page – if they are interested in knowing more.

Ideas on what to share: This is the place to share most of your business updates on Facebook. Consider sharing blogs you have created or curated, quotes that speak to your ideal clients and testimonials from others.

Who should you connect with? People you are interested in doing business with: past, present, and future.

FACEBOOK GROUP

What is it? Facebook Groups make it easy to connect with specific sets of people, like family, teammates or others who share any of your Core Four.

Ideas on what to share: Depending on the purpose of the group you can share many types of things, including: event/project updates, photos, blog posts, quotes or documents; and you can share messages with other group members.

Who should you connect with? People you share things in common with – industry, type of career, passions, etc.

As an example, one of my passions and the focus of my current business is empowering women. My desire to connect with and serve women in leadership across the globe inspired me to start a private group on Facebook. It is a place where women can engage, elevate, and empower each other with articles they have read or written, quotes, images, and whatever else is on their hearts to share. The conversations started light entertaining. Over the years, it has grown to be a platform where REAL discussions are sparked and "in the moment" needs, inspiration, and guidance are asked for and given.

This group is not directly related to my business – however, there are many times I am inspired to write a blog post or interview a fellow member for my Fire Up Chats based on the conversations sparked. 80% of my personal board of advisors is comprised of these brilliant, bold women. (Thank you for your support, #PWe3'ers!)

How can you implement this idea on Facebook?

Have an idea just not sure how to implement? Tweet me @debra11 and tag #FireMeUp11!

TWITTER

What is it? A place to create, learn and share ideas and information instantly, without barriers, or layers of separation between you and those you wish to connect to – any time.

Ideas on what to share: Share your expertise, ask questions and drive traffic to your website or blog posts and those you read. There is a heavy use of hashtags to discover and share on specific topics.

Connections/Audience: Anyone. Friends, peers, leaders, influencers, etc... Find new connections whose problems your business solves or who share passions with you. There are private accounts that require you to request approval.

LINKEDIN

What is it? It is an online community where you connect with other professionals. When you join LinkedIn, you get access to people, jobs, news, updates, and insights that help you excel at what you do. You will also strengthen influence in your industry and procure referrals/recommendations.

Ideas on what to share: This is the place to share your business updates. Consider sharing blogs you have created or curated, quotes that speak to your ideal clients, awards and testimonials from others. Always keep your profile freshened up - even while you are currently employed. This practice not only keeps your information up-to-date, it keeps your profile relevant and top of mind with thought-leaders, recruiters, and potential business partners/employers. Finally, if you do not have a blog of your own, but desire to become a thought-leader in your industry, consider publishing posts on LinkedIn.

Who should you connect with? People you want to do business with or would refer business to. Remember, the core concept of LinkedIn is connecting people you know to each other. Ask yourself, would I refer this person to someone else? If the answer is NO – then there is no need to "LINK".

For instance, if they are colleagues who do the same type of work you do, and you would never refer them business - connect with them on Facebook instead.
Now there are two schools of thought on open connecting on LinkedIn. One camp is focused on connecting with anyone and everyone and the other is focused on connecting with people you know or have a strong mutual connection with in real life.
You must choose what works best for you.

INSTAGRAM

What is it? Photo sharing social network. IG is a camera app that also has filters, frames and other basic editing tools... If you love to take photos – this is definitely a network to consider. IG is also a hashtag heavy network.

Ideas on what to share: Your experiences, favorite quotes or images – mostly taken or created by you. There are also several experts who share tips and tricks on infusing IG into your business promo strategy. One key perk to this app – you can take the photo in IG and share it out to multiple social media sites like: Facebook, Twitter, Tumbler, Foursquare, etc.

Who should you connect with? Anyone. You can follow people you know or try searching the hashtags for your Core Four words to see who shares the same interests. Some accounts are private and require you to request the ability to follow them.

PINTEREST

What is it? A place to share your dreams, expertise, and passions with images from the Internet or your personal/purchase photos on your devices. This is a place for you to truly share your story in a very visual way.

Ideas on what to share/pin: Make a board that represents what you value and one for each of your passions, as appropriate. It is ideal to add your favorite quotes, recipes (food or drink), fashion, and home décor style into your board strategy – those are always a hit on Pinterest.

Who should you connect with? Anyone. You can follow people you know or try searching key Core Four words to see who shares the same interests and style. Consider following your industry influencers and clients to keep up on what they are pinning too!

LIVE STREAMING VIDEO

There are several platforms that have been popping up (and going down) the last couple of years. Instead of reviewing specific sites, here is a general overview of what live streaming video is.

Instead of writing/blogging, people are now sharing their expertise on YouTube, doing Q&As on Periscope, sharing behind the scenes on Snapchat and getting creative on Facebook Live. Friends and fans love it, because they can tune in whenever they like to see you live or catch a replay later.

Here are some ways to use Live Stream Video:
1. Broadcast live events
2. Interviews with influencers, clients, and partners
3. Behind of the scenes of your business
4. How your product is made
5. Quick training segments
6. Q&A sessions
7. Promote upcoming events
8. Announce contest winners
9. Promote recent blog posts/hot topics
10. Tease new products
11. Take your audience "on location"

BLOG

What is it? A platform for you to share your thoughts with written word, photos, videos, podcasts, or whatever your heart desires.

Ideas on what to share: Topics that speak to your Core Four. Write a blog about your passions, write posts that solve your ideal clients problems, share your photography on a photo blog... There is no limit to what you can write about on your own blog, however keeping it somewhat focused on a topic is ideal for your followers.

Who should you write for? You will build an audience based on the topics you write about and by consistently driving traffic to your website's blog.

PERSONAL LANDING PAGES

What are they? Personal landing pages (like about.me) are ideal for those of you who do not have a website right now or ever desire to have one, but still seek a digital identity online. It is also great for those of you who DO have a website or blog – but want an alternative page to tell your story and drive traffic to your content.

Ideas on what to share: You can share your story and personal descriptor words, add your web links, and include all of your social media accounts so people can get to know YOU! Here is mine, as an example: debra11.com

Who should you connect with? You can build an internal community of anyone else who is on the platform!

REVIEW AND DISCOVERY SITES

What are they? Sites like Yelp! and Foursquare/Swarm allow you to share your passions and community expertise by checking in, leaving tips and recommendations, and sharing your feedback out on other social media streams.

Ideas on what to share: Your favorites in every category from restaurants to theatres. If you are a #Foodie – be sure to check-in when you dine at your favorite restaurants in town, leave a tip or review, share it on social media, and later include a link to it in your profile when you blog about the meal. The same goes for your love of wine, dogs, yoga, hiking, etc.

Who should you connect with? You can build an internal community of anyone else who is on the platform. Start by following your friends and add people as you start engaging on one another's posts.

Now that you have a general idea of what happens where, choose one you do not know much about and Google it. Take some time to find out who is spending time there (search: "social media platform demographics"), choose one where YOUR target audience is, and add in that new platform to your social media strategy!

Shine your light.
Share your journey.
When you are courageous
you create a *spark*
that *ignites* and inspires
others to be *brave* !

debratrappen.com

104

Chapter 8
Authentic Online Engagement

"Owning our story and loving ourselves through that process is the bravest thing that we will ever do."
- Brené Brown, Ph.D

Simply put, online engagement should not be a passive experience. Rather than waiting for people to reach out to you, proactively engage with others. In this chapter, we will review some of my all-time favorite tips to take your engagement to an 11.

We will dig into how the photos you choose, the words you use, and the way you engage – MATTERS!

Fire Up Tip 1: Choose Your Profile Photo Wisely

When was the last time you updated your profile photo across your social media accounts? Can you remember or has it been a LONG time?

MAKE SURE TO CHECK AND CONFIRM IT LOOKS LIKE YOU!

If you have changed your hairstyle or have had SEVERAL birthdays since that photo was taken – update it. NOW. Pretty please.

If you are a 55 years young, newly blonde, brilliant beauty today, don't lose out on meeting a fantastic connection because they were looking for a brunette with curly hair or someone in her early 40's! ;)

Seriously now. Having a photo that is 20 years old is NOT a great first impression or positive experience with you. Do you REALLY want someone to meet you for the first time and their first thought to be – "Oh my, she sure looks older in real life!"?

No, I didn't think so.

By the way... this also goes for those overly "photoshopped" photos!

Last (and typed with lots of respect and love) let's talk about your pets and babies.

I know many people adore their pets and babies. Mine dogs are my little furry loves, too. However, unless you are planning to send them in your place to network at the party or rock out a business contract negotiation – please make sure your face is your profile pic.
If you want your pooch or kitty in a front and center position – make them your **COVER PHOTO** instead.

So, please jump over to your social profiles (at least the ones you are active on and/or use for business), confirm your photo is updated, and then PASS THIS TIP ON. (wink)

Fire Up Tip 2: Review Your Contact Info

One of the biggest mistakes I see on social networks isn't just WHAT connections post. Shockingly, it is NOT making it EASY to research and connect from a Facebook (or any social media platform) profile!

Yes. It sounds crazy, but it is true.

I have lost count of how many times I've gone to Facebook to find an email or phone number of an online connection and had to do a web search. Ugh. (Yes, you can send a private message on Facebook, but many people never check that inbox OR the infamous "other" inbox, for that matter!)

If you don't really want to use your main email or mobile number – you can add a general email address and/or a Google Voice number so that people can still reach out to you. Many of the social media sites also give you all sorts of other "contact info" options.

For instance, Facebook allows you add your Twitter and Instagram handles; and offers space to add website links so you can easily share your links to LinkedIn, Blog, Pinterest, etc.

Visit your public Facebook timeline and see what others see when they peek at your ABOUT tab.

(Not sure how? Search "How can I see what my profile looks like to other people?" on Facebook Help for instructions on how to see your public timeline.)

Repeat this process on all your social media platforms. Ask yourself: "What is the experience my online connections have if they look up my contact info?"

You will likely find that there are areas you can improve and update.

Fire Up Tip 3: Handles And Hashtags

What is a "handle" and how do you choose it?

Your handle is your online username. It is the "name" you choose to follow the @ on your Twitter or Instagram account or the name you choose to put after / in your custom URL's on sites like Facebook, Pinterest or LinkedIn.

It is ideal if you can secure your full name for your personal accounts and your company name for your business accounts. Even if you do not USE IT, register it just in case you want to in the future.

Have a hard to spell or pronounce name? Choose something easier that speaks to YOU. My affinity for the number 11 is my guide. Whenever possible I secure "debra11" as my username on all platforms, in addition to grabbing "debratrappen" for future use.

NOTE: Please avoid using your "profession" as or in your main handle. If you make divine cupcakes today and choose @GFCupcakeGal THEN decide to open a wine shop, plan weddings, or sell real estate – your handle will not make sense to your new followers.

If you want to choose or make a change to your handle, check out: namechk.com to find out where it is still available!

Fire It Up To 11 Tip:
Keeping your social media handles and usernames consistent and simple will elevate your engagement and expand your reach!

What is a hashtag and how do you choose it?

Hashtags are an easy way for people to categorize, discover, and join conversations on a particular topic. A hashtag is used to highlight keywords or topics within a post, and can be placed anywhere within a post. Not every single platform uses #hashtags (yet), so please be sure to use them appropriately.

If you are trying to figure out what hashtags you want to use, ask yourself a simple question:

What conversations do I want to spark or join?

Think of #hashtags like your personal brand keywords. If you are passionate about youth justice, gluten-free living, football, or wine - then those are the conversations you want to join in online. Find people talking about those topics by adding a hash/number symbol # in front of the terms, like: #youthjustice, #GFLiving, #NFL, #wine... you get the idea.

Do a little research on similar hashtags being used in those conversations on sites like hashtagify.me – then jump into the social stream with those keyword hashtags and start a conversation.

Fire Up Tip 4: ENGAGE PROGRESSIVE POWER!

This is one of my favorite tips. Normally, when I teach this concept in person, I ask people to close their eyes and imagine this scenario. For OBVIOUS reasons, I would love for you to keep yours open and imagine this:

You are out on a walk with friend. You look up and see the most magnificent sunset happening over the lake in your neighborhood. You pull out your phone, snap a few photos and pop it back in your pocket... until you get in your car! You are super excited to share the gorgeous photo you took, so you fluff it up with a filter or frame – and POST IT on a social platform like Facebook, Google+, or Instagram.

THEN YOU WAIT.

What are you waiting for – in this moment?
Yes! You are waiting for your first **LIKE** on the photo.

When you see it – it feels GOOD, doesn't it? Each like after that brings a smile to your face.

THEN, someone makes a **COMMENT** – maybe something like this: "Gorgeous sunset! Thank you for sharing it! or "This is one of my favorite quotes, too!"

Oh my goodness, now THAT evokes an even stronger emotion than the like, right? When someone takes the 6 seconds of time to leave that comment – **you FEEL special and connected.**

NOW, imagine you come back in a few hours and see a friend has **SHARED IT on their timeline!** Admit it, you do a little happy dance – even if it is just in your head.

When a friend loves our photo so much they want to share it with their world – that means something special to most of us.

It is also important to engage on the comments people leave on your post. If they took the time to leave thoughts, be sure to LIKE their comment. This is like saying "I read this."... If it inspired a thought then RESPOND back.

PLEASE.

PLEASE.

PLEASE.

Stop the "post and run" on social media.

This behavior is like hosting a cocktail party, decorating the house, opening the front door, and then running up to hide in your room all night! When you start a conversation online, be sure to check in and respond throughout the day.

Now, your mission, should you choose to accept it:

DO THIS FOR YOUR FRIENDS!

Be the connection that not only LIKES a post/pic, but comments and shares – when appropriate. It is a simple way to spread joy on social media AND authentically, intentionally take your engagement to an 11!

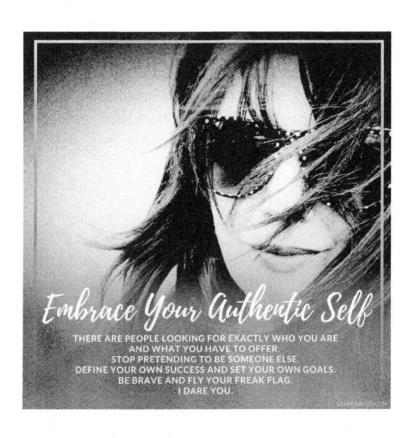

Embrace Your Authentic Self

THERE ARE PEOPLE LOOKING FOR EXACTLY WHO YOU ARE
AND WHAT YOU HAVE TO OFFER.
STOP PRETENDING TO BE SOMEONE ELSE.
DEFINE YOUR OWN SUCCESS AND SET YOUR OWN GOALS.
BE BRAVE AND FLY YOUR FREAK FLAG.
I DARE YOU.

Chapter 9
Golden Rule = Give First

"It takes 20 years to build a reputation and five minutes to ruin it. If you think about that, you'll do thing differently." – Warren Buffet

Serve + Amplify + Engage

If you want to amplify your own voice and figure out your focus, I'm going to give you a piece of advice that may see counter productive – at first. One of the most important things you can do is to follow the golden rule online and "serve, amplify and engage with others **FIRST**"!

I've been sharing a lot about the importance of finding and nourishing YOU -- YOUR values, passions, and purpose. While it is key to know who you are – from the inside out - it doesn't stop there. You have to learn about, love on, and serve others, too.

When you choose to take time to look up and around, with a positive mindset and grateful attitude, the awe-filled moments are limitless. When you go out into the world (and that includes the digital world) you will find beautiful stories, magnificent sayings, amazing products, spectacular people having interesting conversations, and so much more you can engage with and in! You need to jump into THOSE posts. Why? You want to connect with the influencers and tastemakers in your industry or areas of interest. To secure a place for yourself at the table, you are going to need to do some work introducing yourself to them, but not making it all about you. That can be tricky.

Using social media platforms as a megaphone for your "ME" message is easy to do, but is irritating, harmful to your mission to connect with people and damaging to your online reputation. One of the worst things for your personal brand (or your business/career) is to get a rep as someone who just blathers on, posts only about him/herself and doesn't pay attention to what anyone else is saying. *So, don't be that person.*

You will grow and nurture a better reputation by participating respectfully on blogs and in social media conversations. Focus on sharing those influencers and your connection's tweets, pins, and social updates.

However, you don't have to be a wallflower. When you are your fabulous, friendly, passionate self it does two things...

First, it establishes you as a thoughtful person who is generous, fun to connect with, and interested in learning from others. Yay, you!

Secondly, this behavior also helps establish you as a go-to person in your field or industry. You are not only being friendly and sharing others' tweets and statuses; you're also becoming a curator of what's new and interesting. People will start to follow you because of your ability to roundup the best of what's happening in your industry. Double win!

Fire Up Story:

Meet Lisa Archer, CEO of Live Love Homes. Lisa exemplifies the concept of GIVE FIRST. If you follow her on social media – you can't miss her LOVE for and commitment to the communities she serves. I asked her to share one of her "giving adventures" and she, of course, was happy to share.

"At Live Love Charlotte we have launched a division where we give back to our military called Live Love Veterans - in 2013. The first year we had our event where we honored our Veterans at a Carolina Panthers Monday night football game with a tailgate. We also had a canned food drive. In 2014, we had an Angel tree where we collected over 50 gift cards for our disabled Veterans and their families. It has been such a blessing and an honor to love on those that have sacrificed so much."

ASK YOURSELF THIS:
What causes are you passionate about that you can GIVE to AND SHARE what is important to you – all in one?

Here are some social media tips to help you GIVE MORE to your connections:

Facebook:
- o Set up FRIEND LISTS and an INTEREST LIST of the influencer business pages you want to listen to. *(There are list category suggestions at the end of this chapter!)*

- o Check the lists a few times a week, use the progressive power of engagement (Like, Comment, Share) and amplify their message throughout the year.

Twitter:
- o Set up TWITTER LISTS with the specific connections you want to listen to. Start with one with the influencers in your business/industry and another to keep up with others who share your personal passions and interests.

- o Check the lists a few times a week, engage with them and retweet the tweets that resonate with you.

- o If you make your list public, the person will know they have been added to your list and that can trigger another opportunity to connect with them.

- o Also, strive to have 40% of your tweets a combination of retweets (RT) or replies (@ is the first symbol in your tweet). **This shows you share, engage AND listen!**

LinkedIn:

- o TAG your connections when you are sharing their posts or articles about them. Tagging is so underutilized on the platform and it is such a great way to promote and serve your connections

- o Choose one person a week and give them a fabulous, unsolicited recommendation. This is magical.

- o If you don't use LinkedIn often, put an appointment on your calendar to check in on your LinkedIn notifications to keep up to date on your connections careers and stay top of mind with them.

8 LIST CATEGORIES TO INSPIRE YOURS:

To keep things uniform across your social channels, use the same categories for your lists and tags.

1. A+ Champions
2. Personal Friends
3. Family
4. Clients
5. Prospects
6. Collaborators
7. Industry Connections
8. Influencers

Start building your lists today and let the purposeful engagement and connection begin to flow naturally. It feels so amazing when you come from a place of SERVICE first...

Enjoy, my friend!

When we choose to take
time to look up and around,
with a *positive mindset* and
grateful *attitude* , the
awe-filled moments are
limitless!

DEBRATRAPPEN.COM

Chapter 10
Amplify Your Voice

"As you prepare your content for each social channel, do not over-think your posts. Keep them short, sweet, and easy to share!" –Rebekah Radice

You have worked diligently on becoming part of the content-sharing community, added value to (and sprinkled the progressive power philosophy in) social media conversations, commented on blogs and participated in many thought-provoking chats along the way.

At the same time, you have to think about positioning yourself as a knowledgeable member of the industry with the blog posts YOU produce. Creating and sharing content that represents your Core Four, industry, and hot topics will promote engagement, provoke debate, attract ideal connections and inspire shares!

Now it's time to work on amplifying YOUR voice. Here are 5 Fire Up Tips to help you make this happen.

Fire Up Tip 1: Create A Content Calendar And Promotion Strategy

Put together 22 topics you want to blog about in the next 12 months. These should be topics you are passionate about, answer problems you/your business solve, etc. To start, schedule out time to write a blog post for each topic, then create a short video message, haikudeck.com presentation, and/or design a fun visual meme/quote to share for each post with programs like canva.com or the WordSwag app.

This will create at least one piece of custom content every single week with your point of view attached to it. 22 blogs turn into 66 or 88 pieces of sharable content. You can do it all in one week, quarterly, or monthly... however, the farther in advance you create the content – the better.

20% of your content time should be spent creating the content and 80% should be promoting it!

Fire Up Tip 2: Add Social Follow And Share Buttons On Your Website/Materials

MAKE IT EASY for your audience to share and connect with you online. Include social calls-to-action that show people where they can find you on social media. Also install plugins on your blog that allow your audience to share content, and/or opt in to follow your blog RSS feed. Make sure this info is everywhere from your home page and your blog posts, to your email marketing messages and printed materials you give out at open houses, events, conferences, and so on.

Fire Up Tip 3: Customize Your Message Based On The Platform

While you are creating and sharing fabulous content, think of WHEN you are putting it up and how it looks.

For the love of all things social media – PLEASE use the right language on each platform... and stop the generic auto-posting! Each social media platform has a preferred "style" and better times to put your posts out there. Analyze your social media analytics to find out when you should be posting and how to optimize for maximum shares.

(Not sure how to figure this out? Just pop on Google and search "when is the best time to post on _____?" There are plenty of experts who can guide you through this!)

Bottom line: Treat each piece of content according to where it is going so it resonates with that specific audience. The more custom you make it, the more likely to spread.

For example:

Facebook audiences are mainly people who know, like and trust you, the length of posts permitted allows space to share your thoughts – at length and visual posts with photos and videos get fantastic engagement.
Hashtags are acceptable and URL's don't require a www. or http:// to perform.

Twitter requires you to be short and sweet. If you want people to share (retweet) your tweet – keep your characters to 111 or less! Also, you can and should let your sass and sizzle shine. You need to attract attention in seconds.
Hashtags and links are heavily used and URL's don't require a www. or http:// to perform.

LinkedIn is a place for you to shine your knowledge so instead of cutting/pasting a mere link to the content, use the ample character allotment and give YOUR point of view on the post. As mentioned in chapter 7, you can also publish your own posts here to really get your point of view across.
Hashtags are not used on this platform.

Fire Up Tip 4: Implement A Guest Blogging Program

Put together a list of 6-11 bloggers you love to read, share and who also compliment your message. Message them to find out if they would be interested in being part of your guest blogging program. It could be as simple as you each write 2 blog posts for each other in the upcoming 12 months and commit to a simple, minimum social media promotion strategy.

If you put together a team of 6 bloggers – that is another 12 pieces of fresh content on your blogs and tons of conversation in your social streams.

Fire Up Tip 5: Interview Industry Influencers

Embracing change, leveraging social media, and truly leading by example starts with interviews. (The next one will be published on Friday this week, so stay tuned!)

Consider interviewing one of two ways:

Schedule a G+ a LIVE Interview:
Be sure to have your questions prepared ahead of time to show respect for their time. This option is great when you have never met the person in real life. You will "virtually" get a flavor for who they are and, of course, be able to connect a bit more "face to face"!

Do your best to schedule a video chat, however, if you must do a phone interview, go for it.

Email Your List of Questions:
This option is great if you know the person or they have a wickedly wonky schedule since it allows them to answer the questions whenever they are available.

Once you have the blog post or interview answers together, here are some tips:

- o Format the posts the same way –every time. Your audience will start to recognize and look for them.
- o Create a special hashtag for those posts so that you can easily track them online. Include it in the post title.
- o Don't assume interviewees will promote their post and then get disappointed when they don't. **ASK them to assist you in promoting it to their community.**
- o Be sure to tag them when YOU promote the post. Getting it on their radar, in this manner, nearly guarantees they will amplify it to their community!

The best way to amplify your voice and grow your online audience is by fostering a connected, engaged community.

The more your entire follower-base collaborates and connects "in the stream", the more exposure your voice and social presence receives. Not only that, when you consider how most social media platform's algorithms work, the posts that receive the most engagement receive the most exposure in the main feed. When you create content your audience is inspired to engage on AND you personally spark and continue the conversation online you amplify your messages and, ultimately, your voice!

If you want others to help you amplify your voice, make your messages worthy of sharing. Be different. Stand out from the crowd. Be YOU!

I strongly believe YOU should be in charge of your personal social media posts and engagement, however hiring someone to help you manage blog (schedule guest bloggers, for example) and keep your stream filled your content - new and repurposed- is an excellent option for the busy entrepreneur.

Want to chat about these tips?
Tweet me @debra11 and include #FireMeUp11!

If you want others to help you *amplify* your voice, make your messages worthy of sharing. *Embrace being different.* Stand out from the crowd.

Be You!

DEBRATRAPPEN.COM

Chapter 11
Flourish with Focus

"Create the highest, grandest vision possible for your life, because you become what you believe." - Oprah Winfrey.

There is a lot to do when you are defining and designing the best version of YOU, your brand and a fabulous niche focus for yourself and your business. It is easy to get overwhelmed by it all and think you have to magically morph into a magnificent, magnetic multi-tasking machine! (Wow! Say that 11 times fast!)

Before you go any further – STOP trying to do it all – ALL AT ONCE.

Take a deep breath.

In fact, stop the senseless hustling all together. Yes, I said it (well, typed it). Stop multi-tasking and living a hurried, harried life. Slow down and find your focus.

Choose what you WANT in this season and DO THOSE THINGS.

In order to move from mediocre existence to a FIRED UP, flourishing life and business - you must focus on your priorities.

F-O-C-U-S and implement
ONE thing at a time!

Flourishing is the result of prioritizing, pursuing and experiencing a life filled with memorable moments that ignite you.

Flourishing is realized when you are nurturing your relationships, enjoying what you have, striving to fulfill your purpose, and reaching your potential.

Flourishing is about having a career or business you are inspired to pour into each and every day.

Flouring requires you to give something up and create a margin for what matters. You will have to say no MORE and prioritize based on your values, vision, and version of success you have defined.

Simply put, if everything is a priority,
then nothing really is.

Flourishing also requires you to be consistent.

Consistency will help you effortlessly live your life out
LOUD, share your story, gain influence, nurture
relationships, build a successful brand/business and
ultimately serve and care for the people who are
looking for you!

Taking time to be consistent and
focus is worth the investment.

Flourishing

is the result of *focusing* on,
prioritizing, and pursuing a
life filled with *people*
and *experiences* that

ignite you!

DEBRATRAPPEN.COM

Wrapping it UP!

It was my heart's desire to share tips and truths with you to guide, empower, and infinitely inspire you on your Fire Up! Journey.

I pray this book has helped your uncover your unique greatness, get you out of your own way, and ignite your soul to confidently go after your dreams fearlessly, fiercely, and with a fire that sparks everyone around you.

Before we end our time, I would like to share some sassy reminders to keep you on track! Visit these when you need a spark to reignite you, too!

Fire Up Reminder 1:

Take time to revisit your Core Four and focus on developing and nurturing yourself to 11. Start with once a month, then quarterly, and ultimately – make this part of your "annual" planning session.

Fire Up Reminder 2:

Print out your value, soultank, and purpose WORDS. Post them on your bathroom mirror, on your closet door, at your desk, in the laundry room – choose a place you spend quality time.

Fire Up Reminder 3:

Be intentional about your social media presence and engage, elevate, empower, educate, and entertain others while sharing your Core Four.

Fire Up Reminder 4:

Take time to turn off your technology and focus on planning, implementing, assessing, pivoting, and taking your plans to 11.

Fire Up Reminder 5:

Take time to craft magnificent, magnetic relationships and focus on being present, honoring your loved ones, and elevating your relationships to an 11.

Fire Up Reminder 6:

Be sure to define your own version of success. This will help you banish negative self-talk, comparing yourself to others and a myriad of other self-inflicted distractions keeping you from living your life out loud!

Fire Up Reminder 7:

Implement what you have learned in this book and FOCUS on the elements of your signature formula for flourishing - your business and LIFE will go to 11.

Fire Up Your Moxie!

My final gift to you is MOXIE to inspire you! Post these words on your walls, mirrors, fridge, phone, laptop, and beyond to keep YOU fired up!

YOU are born an original...
Don't live like a copy.
Find your voice.
Embrace your uniqueness.
YOU are here for a purpose.
Define it. Visualize it.
Sparkle. Shine. Inspire.

• • •

Vividly IMAGINE it
Visually CREATE it
Faithfully PRAY on it
Whole-heartedly DESIRE it
Deeply BELIEVE it
Passionately ACT upon it and GET READY for it!

• • •

Get up. Stand up. Hands up.
Now, lift your voice up.
Repeat this: I'm unstoppable & I'm worth it!
Now, go get it!

Dream big.
Do your best work.
Visualize the finish line.
Celebrate your successes.
Sprinkle your sparkle!

• • •

pssst...
Smile when you wake up.
Seize and savor each moment.
Define and declare your success.
Give yourself Grace.
Be Fierce. Be Feisty.
Be Fabulous. BE FEARLESS.
Embrace change.
Sprinkle blessings.
Give encouragement.
Empower others.

• • •

Today is a new day.
Embrace the fresh start.
Mistakes don't define you.
Shake off the shame.
Learn the lessons.
Remember, failure is not your final destination...
Get ready to live your life OUT LOUD!

You may be able to fake smarts, attitude, or
experience online.
However, you can't fake consistency.
Put in the time.
Do the work.
Reap the rewards!

• • •

Repeat after me...
Today is going to be magnificent day!
Divine things are going to happen to you and for me.
It is my time to shine.
The best is still to come!

• • •

Be fearless.
Let people call you crazy.
DREAM BIG and Take Action.
Stop pretending.
Embrace who you are.
You are fully equipped to fulfill your purpose!

• • •

When you embrace your authentic self, you have no
competition!

There is no shame in caring about what others think of you. The key is not letting it validate your magnificence or dimming your sparkle!

• • •

Not everyone is going to want, like, except, or know how to receive your energy. Those you are meant to serve WILL. Make peace with that and keeps sprinkling your magic!

• • •

Surround yourself with people who reflect who you want to be and how you want to feel. Energy and attitudes are contagious!

• • •

People inspire you or they drain you.
Choose them wisely.

• • •

No one has the power to determine
your value except for you!
Stop focusing on limiting beliefs.
Embrace your self-worth!

Shine your light.
Share your journey.
When you are courageous,
you create a spark that ignites
and inspires others to be brave!

• • •

You don't need a perfect plan.
BREATHE. Have faith. Let go. Let God.

• • •

Don't let your fears hold you back. Elevate your
thinking. And power your purpose. Live your life out
loud and with joy!

• • •

You were born with a PURPOSE.
You woke up today, brilliant and feisty.
Know what that means?
THERE IS MORE.
You still have amazing things to achieve,
relationships to build and nurture,
mountains to conquer,
a brilliant purpose to fulfill.
You are ready. Be brave.
Inspire your world.
Fire UP!

When focusing on where you have been is no longer interesting to you, you are finally able to move forward and embrace success. Celebrate!

You will also find them on my website: debratrappen.com/moxiememo

Let me know which ones resonate the most with you by pinning them, tweeting me @debra11 and, as always, please use the hashtag #FireMeUp11!

xxoo

Additional PRAISE...

Here are some additional perspectives from amazing people who have worked with Debra...

"Debra is the master and asking questions and truly getting to the bottom of things like values, mission and niche so that you can create something truly unique to you. When you work with Debra, you realize that no matter what industry you are in and how crowded it might feel, you have your own unique set of gifts and talents that allow you to succeed and set yourself apart. Debra is masterful at helping people shift from fear and competition to embracing who they are and building on that from a place of abundance."

\- Nicole Mangina
Real Estate Agent and Business Mentor, Nicole Mangina Inc,

"During the short time I shared with Debra she took my passion, my wife's passion and our businesses to 11! I now have more business just from the life changing words she shared. What Debra offers isn't just great material, but a lifetime of amazing life changing tips that will take your success and business to 11."

\- Brandon Couch
CEO/Founder, BC Creative Media Marketing Solutions

"Debra has helped me face some major growth spurts in my business life and personal life. She was able to show me ways to use the changes I was going through to make positive decisions that would help me accept the growth I was facing. It was overwhelming and I tend to shy away from taking compliments about things I'm doing. She taught me to embrace that with more grace. Debra is a gift. She listens intently to help walk you through to realize the answers you were seeking. She helps you find your strengths and how to deal with any weaknesses. Debra is filled with compassion and no holds barred truth telling. She isn't telling you what you want to hear but telling you what you need to hear."

- Rosemary Buerger
Real Estate Broker Associate, Coldwell Banker

"Just wanted to let you know how your Fire Up program really helped me prioritize my core values and goals. I got off to a rocky start in January so I decided to do a "re-do" of my goals for the year... The best part of your program is allowing me to pivot as needed, as life changes and goals need to be adjusted. I don't see your Fired Up Goals as just a one year goal setting exercise. I see this as an outline for my life's third act journey and to help me see the path to being the best me I can be!

Lisa Dunn
Casa Bella Realty Group

About The Author

Debra Trappen is the Head of Sass and Moxie at debratrappen.com. She founded the firm to help growth-minded leaders FIRE UP, uncover who they are, and become the best version of themselves. This translates into a life, brand, business culture, and attitude that all shine online to attract ideal connections, grow influence and build a prosperous business that fires you up! Engaging, elevating, and empowering women are significant focuses – professionally, personally, and philanthropically.

A sought-after speaker, trainer and author, Debra's been spotlighted on platforms, podcasts and publications across the globe.

When she is not igniting an audience on stage or creating in her studio, you will find her walking her pups or wine tasting with her husband and besties.

Debra offers inspiration and training through Fire Up workshops, books, webinars, keynote talks, books, eCourses, podcasts, and more.

Learn more: debratrappen.com

Hire Debra To Speak

Interested in booking Debra to speak at your next event or conference?

Want to host a Fire Up! retreat, workshop, or webinar for your company, industry association, local network, or business group?

Check out some of her talk topics here:
debratrappen.com/fire-up-talks

Send a note here:
debratrappen.com/connect

Listen to her podcast here:
debratrappen.com/fireuppodcast

Get Connected

You will find her by her handle @debra11 on these social media sites:

My Brilliant Notes:

_____

_____

_____

_____

_____

_____

_____

_____

_____

My Brilliant Notes:

_____

_____

_____

_____

_____

_____

_____

_____

My Brilliant Notes:

_____

_____

_____

_____

_____

_____

_____

_____

_____

My Brilliant Notes:

My Brilliant Notes:

My Brilliant Notes:

My Brilliant Notes:

My Brilliant Notes:

_____

_____

_____

_____

_____

_____

_____

_____

My Brilliant Notes:

_____

_____

_____

_____

_____

_____

_____

_____

_____

My Brilliant Notes:

_____

_____

_____

_____

_____

_____

_____

_____

_____

Enjoy your Fire Up journey, my friend!_
xxoo,

I will leave you with the very first
#MoxieMemo I wrote...

Coffee in my mug.
Big girl panties on.
Swing in my step.
Smile on my face.
Twinkle in my eye.
Glitter on my *lips.*
Sparkle in my wand.
Moxie mission accepted.
Watch out world...

Here I Come!

DEBNATRAPPEN.COM

Made in the USA
Las Vegas, NV
04 February 2022

43075355R00095